UP YOUR ORG

A GUIDE TO HELP

STUDENT LEADERS THRIVE

TAWAN PERRY

COPYRIGHT NOTICE

PUBLISHER'S NOTE

Due to the dynamic nature of the Internet, any web addresses or links contained in this book may have changed since publication and may no longer be valid. This publication is designed to provide accurate and authoritative information in regard to the subject matter covered. It is sold with the understanding that the author and publisher are not engaged in rendering legal, accounting or other professional services. If you require legal advice or other expert assistance, you should seek the services of a competent professional.

TABLE OF CONTENTS

TO ALL STUDENT LEADERS

As a former student leader, I know how challenging being a student leader can be. I've created this book to help you be the best that you can be. It's a blueprint for how to be a successful leader. This book covers critical topics such as how to plan campus events, how to recruit members, how to budget, and how to inspire your peers. Whatever your position is in the organization, I guarantee this book takes your student leadership skills to the next level!

Student leaders will also discover:

How to run more efficient, fun meetings that still get things done

How to get buy-in, even from apathetic students

Effective ways to partner well with administration and other campus organizations

Ways to create a more inclusive and safer campus community

How to create dynamic programs that will be well attended – even on a shoestring budget

Creative ways to re-energize your student organization in the best and worst of times

This innovative book is perfect for:

☑ Student Government Associations

☑ Greek officers

☑ Resident Assistants

☑ Orientation leaders

☑ Club officers, members and advisors

Thank you for your investment in this book and your trust in me to lead you forward.

Tawan Perry, M.Ed.

INTRODUCTION

Hello and Welcome! Thank you for investing in this book. Notice I didn't say purchase.

It's obvious that you know how to make good investments. First, you have chosen to improve your leadership skills. Second, your investment in this book will not only enhance your leadership skills, but also help you to get the most from your student leadership experience.

Everyone can benefit from this book: aspiring student leaders, seasoned student leaders, officers, and even advisors. It's a blueprint to show student leaders how to be a successful campus leader and also avoid some of the common mistakes that student leaders make.

Whether you're involved in SGA, Greek Life, or if you're thinking about getting involved on your campus, this book is packed with information and tools to assist you in becoming a great student leader. It's a hands-on guide all about leadership development and how to get you there efficiently.

In order to get the most from this exceptional guide, read it several times and continue to reference it again and again as you improve your leadership skills. Additionally, take time to think about **Things to Consider** at the end of each chapter.

Wishing you and your organization the best,

Tawan Perry, M.Ed.

CHAPTER 1

Are You a Sellout?

"Unless commitment is made, there are only promises and hopes; but no plans." Peter F. Drucker

A few months ago, I had the pleasure of being the keynote speaker for a statewide student leadership conference in Durham, N.C. It was an incredible experience and opportunity! After the speech I had an opportunity to speak with both SGA leaders and advisors, and one of the questions I was repeatedly asked about was one of the topics from my speech.

The subject was the question, "Are you a sellout?" In the speech I talked about being a sellout for your student organization. In reality, we all sell out to something, but many of us sell out for the wrong reason. Now, don't get me wrong, I know we all have our quirks and vices, but I'm talking about selling out to the idea that we can't achieve our dreams.

The irony of being the keynote speaker is that I had to sell out in order to have the opportunity to be the keynote speaker. You see, two years ago I made one of the toughest decisions of my life, and that was to leave the security of my job and pursue my dreams of becoming a professional speaker.

Having no real connections in North Carolina, it was both difficult and exciting. It was also scary. I knew this country was in the middle of a recession, and that most people would have killed for the opportunity to have a job. On the other hand, it was exciting. After years of contemplating going after my dream, I finally decided to go after what I was born to do.

They say the road to success is littered with booby traps and potholes; well, definitely setbacks, disappointments and failures. In my frustration of being unable to connect with student activity coordinators and leaders, Student Government Association advisors and other decision makers, I decided to get in my car one hot summer day and visit as many colleges as possible between Greenville, N.C. and Asheville, N.C., a journey that lasted for a week.

I had an opportunity to meet many great people along the way. Interestingly, I didn't get one single call from a student activity coordinator. However, I did learn of an organization that was looking for workshop presenters. Long story short, I was given an opportunity to present a workshop for the organization that I mentioned at the beginning of my story. To my delight, that same opportunity has led to many opportunities to positively change lives within and outside of North Carolina.

The point of my story is that, in order to achieve success within your student organization, you must be willing to do the things that others are not willing to do. You must be willing to sell out completely. In other words, you must be willing to take risks, try the unconventional, and never take no for an answer.

So the question of the day is, "Are you a sellout?" Life will not give you what you deserve and life will not give you what you desire. Life will only give you what you demand! If you truly want your organization to be the best it can be, you must demand it and have this expectation every day!

As a student leader you have been **called** to improve the lives of your peers and your campus community. Make no mistake; you help in their process of reaching their goals and dreams. This kind of responsibility should never be taken lightly.

So are you a sellout? If not, you should be, because being successful takes an "all or nothing" attitude.

Things to Consider

1. What expectations do you have of yourself and your organization?

2. Based on your organizational preference, how will joining this organization align with your future goals?

3. What areas of improvement will this organization help you to strengthen?

4. How do you plan to serve your fellow students?

CHAPTER 2

Finding the Perfect Student Organization for You

"I am not concerned that I have no place, I am concerned how I may fit myself for one, I am not concerned that I am not known, I seek to be worthy to be known." Confucius

Looking for a way to meet people in college? Think about joining a club. There are tons of student organizations on most college campuses, and all of them have something different to offer members. But choosing which group is right can be challenging for a new student on campus. In this chapter, I'm going to discuss different ways to find the best fit organization for you.

Tip #1: Ask around.

If you're new on campus, you probably won't know about any student organizations unless you're from the area. This means you'll need to do your homework on campus clubs.

It's a good idea to learn all you can about a group before you commit to joining one. For example, ask experienced students which student organizations are the most active on campus and which ones might be best avoided. Also, if you live on campus your resident advisor is a good resource for this type of information.

Tip #2: Attend student organizational fairs.

Most colleges hold some sort of activities fair during the fall semester to introduce new students to the different groups on campus. If you want to join a club, then you'll definitely want to attend the event. Most campus organizations will be there with information about what they do and how to get involved. Club members will also be there, so you can see what kind of people are involved in each organization and determine if you'd be compatible.

Tip #3: Attend several meetings.

General meetings of student organizations tend to be open to anyone. If you're thinking about joining a specific group, find out when they hold meetings and drop in. Especially if it's a larger group, this shouldn't be a problem.

Tip #4: Look online.

If you know what type of organization you'd like to join but aren't sure exactly what is out there, check your school's website. Most colleges have an office of student activities dedicated to managing student programs, so check their website for a list of groups on campus. For example, you may want to join an art group but aren't sure what is available. You should be able to find the names and contact information for all art groups online.

Tip #5: Think about club sports.

Sports groups are great options for people looking to make friends while being active. You don't have to be very athletic to join a club sport. Most groups will train new members, and some club sports, like ultimate Frisbee, are made up of people with varying skill levels. If you want to get involved but are unsure of which group to join, club sports are a good choice.

Tip #6: Extend high school clubs to college.

Some high school groups have college equivalents. If you enjoyed being in a certain organization in high school, do some research to see if there's a similar college group out there for you. For example, student government is an organization that's always found in both high school and college. Also, high school service organizations often have college counterparts.

Remember, if you don't like a club that you join, you can always choose to leave. So you've really got nothing to lose. Go ahead, get out there and get involved on campus!

Make a list of 3-4 organizations you are interested in joining.

1.
2.
3.
4.

Things to Consider

1. Why are these organizations unique?

2. What do you like to do for fun?

3. What gifts and talents do you have to offer?

4. What are you looking for in an organization?

CHAPTER 3

All Students are Leaders

"The starting point of all achievement is desire."
Napoleon Hill

Being a student leader is about more than holding an office or running an organization. It's about being a contributor to campus life, and about realizing that you serve a purpose in your community.

One of the most important jobs that you have as a student leader is helping other students feel more connected to the campus. This is done by advocating for your fellow students, as well as providing them with events and activities that will enrich their collegiate experience.

Student involvement in extracurricular activities is a key component to ensuring higher student retention rates. This is one of the many reasons that student organizations exist.

Don't have misgivings about being a student leader. Many people who get involved in campus organizations have had little or no previous experience. All you really need is an interest in helping your fellow students.

Come as you are; everyone has something to share. You have a special gift to offer to those around you. The service you provide to your campus enriches the lives of your student community and helps to build a better experience for everyone.

So get involved! Make things happen for your organization and for your campus community. Being a leader is not easy, but know that you are not alone. You are all there because you share a common goal in the desire to serve your campus. So be confident and have fun –

you're going to do a great job!

<u>Things to Consider</u>

1. What do you truly value? Why?

2. What is your idea of a student leader?

3. What organizations were you involved in at your last school? What made you join and get involved?

CHAPTER 4

Budgeting

"Never be afraid to do something new. Remember, amateurs built the ark; professionals built the Titanic."
Anonymous

The key to planning your initiatives and programming for the year is understanding your budget. It is important to make sure that your plans align with your available funding. In this chapter, I will discuss some of the basics of managing your group's finances.

Tip #1: Know your numbers.

When you take office, one of the very first

things that must be done is to check your treasury to find out how much money you have on your account. Also, check with your group's advisor to find out if additional funds have been allocated to your group outside of your remaining funds from the previous year. This will give you a good idea of your total assets, allowing you to plan your budget for the coming year.

Tip #2: If necessary, raise funds for the treasury.

All of the events that your group is interested in planning will have some costs associated with it. If your budget cannot sustain many of your other events, then you will need to think of other ideas in order to raise more funds.

There are many fundraising opportunities available. Speak to your advisor to ask about what past groups have done and how profitable each idea has been. You can also ask other members of the group for ideas, and also search the Internet to see what similar organizations have done to raise funds for their groups.

Additionally, for larger-scale events, you may wish to team up with other organizations and co-sponsor some events in order to combine your resources. This will not only make your events more interesting, but partnering with other groups will help to offset event costs, as well as to foster a spirit of goodwill between your respective organizations.

You must also pay your dues even if you're an executive board member. Remember, even the best-planned event cannot become a reality if there is no money in the treasury!

Tip #3: Don't break the bank.

Sticking to your budget is extremely important. Funds are limited for everyone; if you plan to spend more than you have, it will be very difficult for you to get the funds you need later. Early in your planning stages, make sure to get help from your advisor and any other professionals that can offer you advice. Remember that you can't have an event if you can't pay for it. Preparing early in the process will pay huge dividends throughout the year.

You should also be realistic about how you want to distribute the funds for each event. Would your group prefer lots of smaller, lower budget functions, as opposed to one massive event that could potentially cost you all that you have? Both scenarios are a financial gamble, so it's important to know your student membership well and to take their interests into account. You may wish to consider putting these choices to a vote.

Aside from your group's mission, there is nothing more important than the assets that your organization has. In order to make your plans a reality, a careful budgetary planning process is necessary. Just remember to keep your focus on knowing what you have and working within your means.

Also, do not be afraid to ask for help if you need it. Keeping a careful eye on the bottom line can be a lot of work, but when your organization is enjoying an event that everyone has helped to plan, you will see that the end result is well worth the extra effort.

Things to Consider

1. If you hold an executive position, set up a meeting with your advisor and members to discuss the budget.

2. What budgetary challenges do you currently have and how do you plan to solve them?

3. What events will require a small amount of your budget? What big events will require a huge amount of your budget?

4. What events require priority funding? Why?

CHAPTER 5

Goal Setting

"Leaders are made, they are not born. They are made by hard effort, which is the price which all of us must pay to achieve any goal that is worthwhile." Vince Lombardi

Regardless of what your wishes are, the only way that you will be able to achieve them is by establishing goals to help you along your journey. This is also true of your dreams, as well as your everyday responsibilities. If you're feeling stuck along the road to success, try some of the steps below to see if you can find your way back along the path that you're meant to be traveling.

Tip #1: Determine what it is that you'd like to accomplish.

Perhaps you're having a problem that's been bothering you recently, or it's something that you've been trying to resolve for a longer period of time. Or, maybe you're just not sure which direction you need to go at this time. Ask yourself some of these questions: "What do I want?" "What steps do I need to take to get there?" "Are these changes long term or short term?" "What changes would I love to see on campus or at school in general?"

Tip #2: Figure out which outcomes are realistic.

Although the sky should be the limit with goals, you will need to determine whether or not they are feasible, not just for yourself, but for other people as well. Ambition is a great thing, but remember that if your goals aren't grounded in reality, then it's going to be impossible to reach them and disappointing in the end. Stick to the ones that make the most sense.

Tip #3: Break it down.

This is an easy, yet necessary part of goal setting. If the outcome you want seems realistic but difficult, look at it from all perspectives. Try to deconstruct each goal into many smaller, manageable steps. A good way to achieve this is by creating a weekly to-do list that connects to larger goals. With each of these small steps completed, you will get closer to your ultimate outcome.

Tip #4: Make the most of what you have.

Even if your goals seem impossible, if you're breaking them down into small steps, you should also be able to utilize all the resources at your disposal. And when it becomes necessary, always delegate responsibilities to others. Form committees and start routines that will help you reach a common goal.

These tips will help you to stay on track. By keeping regular routines, by delegating responsibilities and being realistic, keeping on top of your goals will be much easier. However, you must realize that with many different challenges, and with multiple opinions going back and forth, it can be easy to get off track from time to time. This happens to everyone.

Time passes quickly, but when you're working to keep everyone motivated and focused, you'll be able to look back proudly at all that you've been able to accomplish.

Things to Consider

1. What are three goals you have for the coming year or current semester/quarter?

   a)
   b)
   c)

2. How do these goals connect to your long-term goals?

3. What steps do you need to take in order to accomplish these goals?

4. What resources will you need to utilize in order to achieve these goals?

5. How do currently go about accomplishing your goals?

CHAPTER 6

Programming 101

"What you want to do, and what you can do, is limited only by what you can dream." Mike Melville

Your student organization depends on programming to help the students feel more connected to the campus community. Therefore, it is vital that your group plan events that will interest your student body. Coming up with interesting ideas is not always easy since each student has different opinions, needs, and expectations. This chapter gives you some ideas about how to get started in organizing activities for everyone. Additionally, the Appendixes give you program examples which have not only been proven to be effective, but also ideas that can work well even on the smallest budget.

Whatever your idea, your programming procedure will probably follow the same basic format. Here are some basic steps toward organizing a great event:

Step #1: Determine what type of event you will hold.

It may seem quite easy to figure out which type of program will be best, but surprisingly, this decision may be one of the hardest to make. Be sure to get plenty of feedback from others during the decision making process. Ask your advisor for some ideas, as well as other members of the group.

Step #2: Reserve the date and venue well in advance.

If you are planning to work with an off-campus vendor (such as a musician, hypnotist, or speaker), make sure that they are available for the date that you want.

Step #3: Consider the setup.

Inform your facilities manager or department about the type of setup your event will require. What size room will you need? Will you need any special equipment? Communicate with all of the other organizations you'll be working with in order to have what you need for your program to run smoothly.

Step #4: Organize responsibilities.

If this is a large-scale event, appoint specific responsibilities to various members. For instance, who will be responsible for marketing the event? Who will be responsible for the food? Assemble teams and give everyone a job to do.

Step #5: Publicize your event.

It may seem difficult, but there are basics

to follow in this step. In short, advertise your event as much as possible. Use all means that are available to you: social media, word of mouth, post flyers on campus, ListServ emails; use campus and local newspapers or radio stations. Ask others for ideas on how to advertise the event as well.

Tip #6: Have a "Plan B" ready to go.

Regardless of how meticulously you have planned your event, there's always a chance that something can still go wrong. In order to ensure that everyone's hard work ends in a great event, be sure to prepare everything as far in advance as possible. Think of "what if" scenarios, and try to form backup plans for them as well.

Remember that holding a great event takes a lot of preparation and even a bit of luck. Even if you don't pack the house for every event, the key is to always do your best to provide your students with options that they will appreciate. A positive attitude, some innovation, and some careful planning will go a long way to providing your fellow students with many memorable, fun, and interesting events.

Things to Consider

1. What events or activities have been successful in the past?

2. How would you improve past program success?

3. What new events/programs would you like to implement at your school? What resources will you need?

4. How many programs do you plan to organize in a month? In a year?

5. What kind of programs do your students need or want? How do you plan to survey your students?

6. What is the best way to attract your students?

7. Afterwards, how do you evaluate your programs?

CHAPTER 7

Running Meetings

"Boredom: the desire for desires." Leo Tolstoy

Every member of an organization is always going to prefer the fun events to the meetings. None of these events would be possible without everyone getting together beforehand to plan and discuss these events. A good meeting should have two important characteristics. They should be both productive and interesting. Here are a few ways to make your meetings more productive and even more enjoyable for everyone involved.

Tip #1: Structure is key.

Try to plan your meetings so that they enable plenty of time for relevant discussions. A more interesting yet unconventional format for this is to set aside the beginning of the meeting to go over new business first and then concentrate on older issues. This enables everything to keep moving forward while getting the meeting off to a more exciting start.

You might also try an ice-breaker to get things off to a fun and interesting start; it motivates people to attend and also helps in team building. Talk about issues that are going on at school, and ask for others to participate. No matter what, keep things moving forward to ensure that everyone present is engaged in the meeting.

Tip #2: Give everyone a voice.

Allow all attendees to participate. Delegate jobs to as many people as possible, and allow each person to give a report or commentary on recent events. This has two benefits. The first is that each person can feel more involved in the meeting, and the second is that all parties involved know what's happening with the other people in attendance.

Bonus advantage: When everyone is kept in the loop, it makes it easier for each member to partner with one another for help if someone needs it. Communication like this can be tremendously insightful and productive.

Tip #3: Meet with purpose.

Nothing is more annoying to a busy person than having someone waste his or her time. The purpose of having a meeting is to get things accomplished. Therefore, if there is no new business to manage, and no new developments in older matters, then you need to determine if it's necessary to meet that week. If you don't need to do so, cancel and spare others the frustration of coming together for no reason.

Tip #4: Manage conflicts wisely.

If you're having a conflict with someone else during a meeting, or as a student leader you notice that two other members are clashing, do not bring it up right away in front of everyone. Instead, after the meeting has ended, take the parties involved outside and discuss it at that time. Try to find out if those people can come to an agreement.

It may not always work, but taking the disagreeing parties aside and talking privately is much more productive and also much less embarrassing than calling them out in front of all the others in attendance.

There are many ways that you can keep your meetings lively and full of purpose. Just because meetings are supposed to be work does not mean that they have to be unpleasant. Remember to keep things moving forward and to stay focused on the common goals of the organization. With just a bit of creativity and planning, your group can make meetings enjoyable and meaningful for everyone.

<u>Things to Consider</u>

1. What are three things you can suggest or do in order to make your meetings more fun and interesting?

   a)
   b)
   c)

2. How do you plan to structure your meeting times?

3. What's the one thing you would do differently if you ran the meeting?

CHAPTER 8

Being a Student Leader on a Commuter Campus

"Leadership is action, not position."
Donald H. McGannon

Student leadership can be challenging in any scenario, but holding the position on a commuter campus comes with its own specific set of challenges. Regardless of the campus location, one of the most difficult tasks a student leader faces is finding new ways to get the students involved. Here are a few ideas to help get you started.

Tip #1: Walk a mile in others' shoes.

Learning to "think outside the box" can be very effective. Try to understand the culture of the people that you're trying to engage. For example, if many students spend time off campus because of family, jobs, or other commitments, find innovative ways to get them coming back when they have the time. Ask for feedback; find out what's important to them, or what would inspire them to spend more time on campus.

Tip #2: Go for instant gratification.

The lack of student involvement often indicates that the student's time is needed elsewhere. If you find that students don't spend much time on campus outside of their classes, hold events that won't take up too much of their time. Place events in convenient locations that are easily accessible to students. Market your events in advance, but also advertise before or during events in order to reach a wider audience.

Tip #3: Accommodate your audience's schedule.

Commuters tend to schedule their education around other parts of their day. Therefore, events that are held during traditional times are not going to provide much of a draw to these students. If you find this to be the case at your school, try scheduling your programming at less traditional times.

Remember, while residential campuses and commuter campuses are different in many ways, the commonality is that all students are there to learn. Many students are not always aware of the events and programs that are offered, so as a student leader it is your job to make everyone feel as though they are a part of the school community.

By learning as much as you can about the students that you serve, you will be doing a great service to everyone. While this can be tough for the student leader in a commuter campus setting, it is possible – and even enjoyable – with a little creativity and a lot of flexibility.

<u>Things to Consider</u>

1. What advantages do you have being on a commuter campus?

2. What programs and events have worked in the past?

3. What programs and events do you have for nontraditional students?

4. What is the greatest need of your students?

CHAPTER 9

So You Wanna be a Club Officer?

"Two roads diverged in a wood, and I... I took the one less traveled by, and that has made all the difference."
Robert Frost

Taking on a leadership role in college can be tough. At times it requires neglecting your studies, and it may force you to miss out on some social activities. But although running a student organization has its challenges, the rewards can certainly pay off.

Working in an executive position of a student organization gives you a taste of what leadership is like in the real world. As a student leader you have a very real chance to make a difference on campus, and it also sets you up nicely for a career after college.

Despite all the benefits of being in charge, not everyone is born a natural leader. Luckily, however, there are some things that even the least likely leader can do to hone their management abilities and become an effective student president, vice president, secretary, or treasurer for an organization.

What does it take to be an effective student leader? Besides talent, it takes effort, well-developed time management skills, the ability to communicate effectively, and a desire to lead. And even if leadership doesn't come naturally, a good dose of effort will make up for it.

Approaching a position with hard work and dedication can make almost anyone into an effective leader. Unfortunately, effort implies sacrifice and discomfort, which is just what you deal with as president of a student organization. To do a good job in a leadership role, you must be willing to give up some nights out with friends and expect to spend long hours developing plans and delegating responsibility for your group.

Good student leaders are masters of time management skills and practically have them down to an art. To excel as president, vice president, or other high position in a student organization, you must learn to balance school, your social life, and maybe a job in your role as student leader. This means that every waking hour counts.

Most good leaders keep detailed schedules, so they know exactly what to do at certain times. If you find yourself struggling with too much to do in too little time, create an hour-by-hour schedule that sets aside blocks of time for each activity.

The best leaders know how to effectively communicate with all kinds of people in any situation. A leadership role requires that you talk to the people in your organization, consult with faculty and advisors, communicate with people outside of your group, and negotiate with members of your larger community.

All of this talking can be too taxing for someone who is not comfortable with public speaking. Most good communicators are friendly and unafraid of meeting new people. Good leaders share these qualities.

While someone can have all the qualities of natural talent, dedication, time management and highly developed communication skills, they can still fail as a leader if they lack the desire to take on a specific role. Therefore, it's crucial that if you want to hold a high position in an organization, that you are effective at your job. Otherwise, taking on leadership responsibilities will make you miserable and you'll probably do a poor job.

So before you run for an office, think about whether you really have a desire to do the job and actually want it. If you do, great! A healthy desire for leadership means you're already halfway there.

Things to Consider

1. Why do you want to be an officer, not president?

2. If you are elected, what's your first course of action?

3. What other existing commitments do you have?

CHAPTER 10

You've Been Elected...Now What?

"Becoming a leader is synonymous with becoming yourself. It is precisely that simple, and it is also that difficult." Warren G. Bennis

So you were voted to lead your campus organization this year and you feel good. You are the boss! But, at what cost? Before you start your new regime, consider these tips to help you get started.

Tip #1: Name your price.

As with all things you do in life, it's important to name your price. Don't take on the challenge of holding an executive position until you are completely sure that you can commit to the position.

One of the many situations I witnessed, both as a student leader and as a college administrator, was students taking on leadership roles and never once considering the time and energy it takes to be a good leader. For example, I once held four presidential positions at the same time. Was I an effective leader? It depended on which of the four organizations you were talking about.

If you decide to take on the responsibility of being a campus leader, consider the time and commitment it will take. If you don't, you will certainly pay a price you might not want to pay.

Tip #2: Have a vision.

Leaders are measured by what they actually accomplish, not by what they just talk about. Once you take office, meet with your fellow officers and advisors and decide what you want to accomplish for the year. It will not be as easy as you might think to set a vision that is both measurable and realistic.

Tip #3: Recruit your supporting cast.

The best leaders always know how to delegate, and in order to do that, you need a team you can trust and have confidence in. Choose wisely and look for qualities in your team that complement each other. Having too much like-mindedness can be a bad thing. Conversely, having too many varying opinions can lead to unnecessary disputes and an unproductive administration. If you inherit a team, the best strategy is to get to know each member and utilize their skills to the best of your ability.

Tip #4: Don't be afraid to fail.

As a leader you must take risks, and if you fail you might be blamed. So what! It comes with the territory. The key is to learn from your mistakes and allow those mistakes to help you become a better leader.

<u>Things to Consider</u>

1. Why would you like to hold an executive position in your organization? In the spaces below, list the pros and cons of holding an executive position.

   Pros:

   a)
   b)
   c)
   d)
   e)
   f)
   g)

   Cons:

   a)
   b)

c)

d)

e)

f)

g)

2. What's your game plan? If you don't have one, who can help you get started?

3. What other existing commitments do you have that may interfere with serving as an officer?

CHAPTER 11

Calling Forth Your Team

"We may have all come on different ships, but we're in the same boat now." Martin Luther King, Jr.

As a student leader, you must understand that your organization is at its strongest when everyone works together as a team. When you first become elected into student leadership, one of your first duties will be to delegate authority to other people on your team. You may wonder what type of people will be the most useful for each position, and whom you can trust for specific jobs.

Here are a few tips to help you determine which types of people you will need in your organization.

Tip #1: Seek people who have diverse opinions.

Surround yourself with many different types of people; this exposes you to diverse opinions and attitudes about getting things done. Don't just choose your friends; try to select people of varying familiarity. If you have too many like-minded people, it will be difficult to see a situation from varying perspectives; instead, your group will only view a small piece of the puzzle. Therefore, make sure you have some diversity to give a much-needed reality check.

A Word of Caution: While you do want to interact with others whose opinions differ from your own, care should be taken that you don't choose people who are so different that arguments get in the way of productivity.

Tip #2: Seek people who have a positive attitude.

Make sure that you choose people who have positive attitudes. In a student organization, there is nothing more draining or difficult than having an organization full of naysayers. You need to work with students who see things in a positive light and who are willing to bring something to the table, no matter how small.

People who have negative attitudes tend to be fearful in taking a stand and are less likely to contribute to the overall well-being of the organization and the school as a whole. However, if you are given a choice between a positive "yes man" who has nothing to contribute, and someone who's perhaps more pessimistic but willing to do the work to make necessary changes, you should give the hard worker a chance to make things happen.

Being positive is important and should be encouraged, but persistence and industriousness will often lead to positivity as well.

Tip #3: Seek people who are willing to honor their commitments.

Student leadership is a commitment and can often require much of your time. It's a juggling act that never ends, so be sure that you're willing to commit to your part of the job. Moreover, you must surround yourself with a team of people who are also willing to honor their commitments.

Some people will agree to participate in multiple organizations, yet all of the projects will suffer because the student has simply bitten off more than he or she can chew. Make sure that all parties involved have the time and the ability to commit to your organization.

Tip #4: Seek people who have connections.

One of the best things you can do for your group is to work with people who are connected to the campus or other organizations in unusual ways. Perhaps they have access to resources that can help the organization. Even if someone doesn't have a special talent or skill, perhaps he or she knows someone through work or family who has connections, whether on or off campus, that can be beneficial to the group.

Keep this idea in mind when assembling people for your team. Sometimes people who have connections to those outside of your institution or organization can be extremely valuable and helpful members of your team. These types of people will help your group achieve many of the goals that have been set for the organization.

However, remember the most important qualification: You must seek people who are as passionate about being in the organization as you are. Even someone with no special talents or skills can accomplish much if he or she has the drive and focus to make things happen.

There is nothing more vital than shared passion for the group's mission. You can achieve great things for the organization if you combine forces and work as a team.

<u>Things to Consider</u>

1. What are the top three qualities you look for in the members of your organization?

    a)
    b)
    c)

2. What is your pet peeve?

3. If you are president or vice president, what criteria will you use to appoint other student leaders?

CHAPTER 12

Your Organization's MVP

"A successful team is a group of many hands but of one mind." Bill Bethel

Who is the most important person in the organization? Before you answer, consider the following story.

In his book, *Teaching the Elephant to Dance: The Manager's Guide to Empowering Change*, author James A. Belasco, Ph.D., tells a story of Dr. Denton Cooley, the famous heart surgeon.

One day, the author followed Dr. Cooley on his rounds. In route to the operating room, the surgeon stopped to talk to a man mopping the hallway. The two men conversed for nearly ten minutes before Dr. Cooley dashed into the operating room. Curious, the author walked over to the man with the mop and said, "That was a long conversation."

The man replied, "Yes, Dr. Cooley and I talk quite often."

Then Belasco asked, "What exactly do you do at the hospital?"

The man replied, "WE SAVE LIVES."

In the best organizations there is no such thing as "them" and "us." There is only "we," everyone working together. In the big picture, everyone has a unique role to fill, everyone holds a piece to the puzzle, and everyone, including and perhaps especially you, makes a difference.

Think for a minute…who is the most important person in the organization? **Everyone.**

One of the greatest misconceptions that people hold is that they don't really impact the lives of others, but that's simply not the case. American environmentalist, Julia Butterfly Hill, wrote this:

"The question is not 'Can you make a difference?' You already do make a difference. It's just a matter of what kind of difference you want to make, during your life on this planet."

The reality is that you make a difference when you least expect it. For example, in 2003 as SGA Vice President, I appointed one of my SGA officers to start a summer program called "And then they were Queens." The purpose of the orientation program was to help prepare incoming first-year female students for the social challenges of college, and also to help them build their self-confidence.

Although I can't take credit for advancing the program, I was told that I was the reason it got started. And now, I can't begin to imagine how many young women this program has helped over the years. In fact, one of the women in the program went on to become SGA president.

As student leaders, you have an immense opportunity each day to build your legacy, but it is always up to you to decide what that legacy will be.

My challenge for you is to ask yourself: **What is my legacy?** Better yet: **What do I do each day to make others feel like they matter?**

Legacy is defined by how we connect with and impact others with our words and deeds. Your legacy doesn't have to be starting a program or starting a revolution.

"The purpose of life is to discover your gift. The meaning of life is to give your gift away." David Viscott

Start to fulfill your purpose, your meaning, your legacy, and make things easy for people by validating them. It's one of the greatest gifts you can ever give someone.

Things to Consider

1. What is one small thing you can do each day to help another student?

2. In the space provided, list your <u>Strengths</u>, <u>Talents</u>, and <u>Gifts</u>:

   -
   -
   -
   -
   -
   -
   -

3. How can you use these talents and gifts to help other people?

CHAPTER 13

What – No Summer Vacation!?
Using Your Summer to Prepare
For What's Ahead

"It's not the will to win, but the will to prepare to win that makes the difference." Paul "Bear" Bryant

Now that you're the boss, did I mention that there is a cost to be paid? While we all can use a restful and quiet summer, as a student leader you are not necessarily afforded such a luxurious opportunity. If you want a successful academic year, you'll be wise to use the summer months to plan ahead. Here are a few tips to help you maximize your planning time.

Tip #1: Honesty is the best policy.

If you were an active member of your organization last year, have an open and honest discussion about what worked and what didn't work so well. This time should not be used to play the blame game, but rather as a time to respectfully discuss where you would like to see the organization go this upcoming year. From past experience, I can tell you that nothing will be more important than honesty as you move forward.

Tip #2: Brainstorm!

Absolute magic can happen if you use this "slow time" to brainstorm every possibility. As student leader you are not just a ceremonial leader, so it's okay to think outside of the traditional norms of your school.

Sure, advisors will require you to do many things, but brainstorming sessions give you opportunities to think creatively of ways to improve your campus community and connect students to your campus. No idea is considered too outrageous as you prepare for the upcoming school year.

Tip #3: Your legacy.

One of the most important questions you can ask yourself as student leader, and to a larger extent as an organization, is just how you plan to define your legacy. In the best of situations, you can choose how you want to contribute to your campus. However, in the worst of situations events sometimes unravel, and they define your legacy to campus.

During my time as SGA Vice President, our legacy was unfortunately defined by the tragic deaths of three students during that year and how we responded to them. As leaders, we did our very best to console the campus and bring back normalcy. By comparison, our predecessors' legacy was defined by them taking strong, proactive roles in their involvement with new buildings being erected on campus.

Your year will be full of both good and bad surprises, but one thing is for certain: You will leave a legacy.

Tip #4: Seek expertise.

One of the biggest mistakes I made during my time as an SGA officer was not getting trained on how to be an SGA vice president. Like everyone else, we all assumed we would learn as the semester moved on. We learned all right, but not the lessons that we wanted to learn.

The biggest lesson I learned was the importance of consulting with student leadership experts to come to our campus and educate us on how to be effective leaders, like how to run efficient meetings, effective ways to connect to the student body, and planning well-attended events. Many of our mistakes could have been avoided had we taken the opportunity to be mentored by an expert. Nothing is worse than leading a campus when you really don't know what you are doing.

"What about your advisors?" you ask. Advisors can certainly give you a level of insight and opinion. But sometimes they can't give you optimum advice because they are too close to the situation to see it from another prospective. Hiring an outside leadership expert will be the best leadership development investment of the year.

To get the best possible outcome from your year as a student leader, use your valuable summer months to honestly discuss your vision for the upcoming year, to brainstorm and think creatively of ways to improve your campus and to connect students, to define your legacy, and to seek expert training. Your efforts, as well as those who advise you, will make the year more enjoyable for everyone and also lessen your stress as a student leader.

Things to Consider

1. Name three things you plan to accomplish over the summer:

   a)

   b)

   c)

2. When and where will your meetings take place?

3. What's your most important issue to address going into the new year?

CHAPTER 14

The First Eight Weeks

"The key is not to prioritize what's on your schedule, but to schedule your priorities."
Stephen Covey

The beginning of the school year can be a hectic time; before you know it, the first two months have already flown right past you. Time moves quickly because you've gotten off to a busy start, and usually you are so preoccupied after settling into school that you lose all track of how quickly time is passing.

Be sure to pace yourself so that you have enough energy for all that life is handing you. The tips below can help tremendously in you winning the race against time.

Tip #1: Learn to say no!

There will be many requests of you as a student leader, and though you may try, no one is capable of doing it all. Choose your battles wisely; the tasks that you choose should be doable as well as important to you. If something doesn't work for you right now, it's okay to refuse and revisit the request later if time permits. For now, just focus on scheduling important items.

Tip #2: Delegate.

If you are an officer in your student organization, you must realize the importance of delegating responsibility, because **<u>no one</u>** can do everything by himself or herself. You're part of a team within an organization, so remember that there are others around who can help lighten the load considerably. **Even if you are in a position that holds more power or responsibility, don't**

make the mistake of believing that you must handle everything yourself. The team is at its strongest when everyone is doing his or her fair share. Hand others the reigns once in awhile, so that you can focus on other issues which need your attention.

Tip #3: Prioritize important items.

You must also ensure that your priorities are where they need to be. Obviously, you should make your academic obligations the most important priority of all. Your organization is important, but it will need to take a backseat to your grades and overall academic health.

Remember that the reason you're in school is to get an education above all else, so don't lose sight of that goal. No matter how many other obligations you may have or organizations in which you participate, your number one job at school is to get a degree. It can be easy to lose sight of this goal when all the little tasks get in the way, but try to keep your schoolwork as your first priority.

Students have many demands on their time, from classes to studying and other personal obligations. Time flies especially fast during your first year of college, but it can also happen to seasoned upperclassmen as well. Whether it's your first year in college or your last, the aforementioned tips mentioned in this chapter will help you to survive the first weeks of your school year and establish habits to hold you in good stead throughout your college career.

__Things to Consider__

1. How do you plan to balance your schedule at the beginning of the school year?

2. What are your priorities?

3. What duties can be delegated in the first eight weeks?

CHAPTER 15

What "First Years" Really Want

"Spread love everywhere you go. Let no one ever come to you without leaving happier." Mother Teresa

As both a former student leader and college administrator, I've seen my share of Welcome Weeks, Orientation, First Year Experience programs, and whatever else they may be called. The one commonality I've noticed at many of these schools is that all first years typically want the same things. It's as universal as Maslow's Hierarchy of Needs theory. In the eyes of student affairs professionals, this may come as no surprise.

There are three essential conditions that first years really want. Of course, I'm no theorist, but I can say that I've worked with enough students to truly see what's obvious. So, here are the top three conditions that I believe first-year students really want...and deserve.

First Years Really Want to Belong.

No matter how apathetic, shy, or disruptive they might be, all students want to belong and know that they matter. The difference between a student graduating and departing from an institution is how well they feel that they are connected.

There are many other reasons why a student might leave, but one thing is for sure. If a student doesn't feel connected to a campus, it will dictate whether or not they excel in their academics, what type of extracurricular activities they get involved in, and determine what type of relationships they develop.

From a disciplinary standpoint this cannot be understated. The same energy it takes for a student to become a disruptive force on campus can also be reversed when the student really understands that they matter.

What can you do to make a student feel like they matter? The answer lies in institutional values. If your institution values money more than students, it will be reflected in your budget and policies. All of us, including institutions, assign money, time and energy to the things we value.

Now, what you can do as a student leader?

The best thing you can do is to get out there and meet your new students! Believe it or not, it's very easy for a student leader to get caught up in their title. Here are a few ideas to get you out in front of the student body:

☑ Hold general meetings.

☑ Attend campus sporting events.

☑ Sponsor events with food and prizes.

☑ Eat in the cafeteria with first years.

☑ Encourage an open door policy.

☑ Host Welcome Weeks.

☑ Ask first years to get involved.

☑ Ask them for their feedback.

<u>Remember</u>: The more they see you as a "regular student," the less intimated they will be by you. And this will increase the likelihood of you making a connection with them.

First Years Really Want Security.

If you ask most incoming students their reasons for going to college, 9 out of 10 will say to get an education so that they can have a career.

While this may be true, and depending upon the institutional culture, these same students will also probably speak to the social experience of college.

A student's choice of institution may very well be due to its social scene (parties). However, having a good time should never be at the expense of their safety or security. I can't tell you how many times my heart has been broken due to the amount of rumored and actual sexual assaults that have taken place on my college campus.

I'm not saying that the institution is completely to blame for a student's behavior, and I'm not saying that the institution should be held responsible for every bad thing that happens on campus. However, I am saying that the last thing a young woman or man would like for the rest of their life is a horrible experience with sexual assault.

When I speak of security, I'm not suggesting that the institution utilize special police officers and attack dogs to shut down social gatherings with underage alcohol consuming parties. But I am suggesting that all campuses (especially residential) revisit the activities of the first two weeks of school. The times when students most need a structured agenda of activities are after hours, that is, after midnight. All first years deserve that much.

What can you do as a student leader?

Perhaps the best thing you can do with first years with regard to safety is to get them well acquainted with the campus culture and rules. I'm not implying that you become the campus police, but as a more experienced student you share in the responsibly of helping first years to transition smoothly.

Here are a few **tips**:

☑ Be a positive role model.

☑ Sponsor a "Midnight Lock-in" the first week of school.

☑ Provide a variety of alternative programs for students who do not wish to engage in the party social scene.

☑ Hold each other accountable to high behavioral standards.

☑ If sexual assaults are an issue, address them publicly.

☑ Debrief first years on the dangers of alcohol and substance abuse.

☑ Partner with social organizations to create safer party environments.

First Years Really Want a Good College Experience.

Make no mistake; all first years really want a good college experience. Sure, some may be at school just to transfer, but during their time there they expect a good experience. Otherwise, they would not attend your institution.

What is the best way to give them a good experience? Get back to the basics. This starts by taking care of those who work directly with students. When your employees love and enjoy working at the institution, it shows. It becomes infectious.

First years are very smart and also very easily influenced. Just "being involved" was not the only thing that made my college experience great. It was also seeing how much faculty and staff members loved working for the institution. They were the reason that I got involved and ultimately chose a career in higher education. Did they agree with every decision that the school made? Of course not, but it was my belief that overall they were very happy.

If you really want to give first years a good experience, provide your faculty, and especially your staff (of course, I'm biased), a great work environment.

What else can you do as a student leader?

Nothing will set the tone greater for a student than seeing student leaders speak highly of their school and displaying campus pride. Conversely, nothing is more deflating than for a first-year student to witness student leaders bash their campus. You may be frustrated with your campus, but that gives you no right to publicly condemn it. And nothing good can come of it.

To create a good college experience for first years, you should:

- ☑ Keep negative comments and opinions private.

- ☑ Sponsor a faculty/staff appreciation event.

- ☑ Survey your first years about what they would like to have happen.

☑ Go on a bi-annual retreat to re-energize.

☑ Provide a good mix of campus events.

☑ Provide programs for nontraditional and commuter students.

Taking a sincere interest in first-year students promotes their sense of security and helps them to transition smoothly on campus. As you welcome your new students, provide them with the important information they will need to feel safe and to become well-acquainted with the campus culture and rules.

Things to Consider

1. What do you believe are the biggest challenges for first years on your campus?

2. How do you plan to address these issues?

3. What events do you have planned for first years?

CHAPTER 16

When Things Fall Apart

"Never look down on anybody unless you're helping him up." Jesse Jackson

There is always excitement at the beginning of each new school year surrounding new opportunities and new possibilities, and no group knows this better than student leaders.

But after all the exhilaration of a new year runs out, and academic, social and extracurricular demands become more hectic, student leaders sometimes find themselves not as motivated to serve. And now, you must help to reignite the flame within them.

Well, look no further for ways to reenergize student leaders. Here are two sure-fire tips to get your students reconnected in no time!

Tip #1: Recommit to "Why."

Often, the goals and objectives that you established at the beginning of the year are no longer applicable. Maybe your organizational structure changed, or you must address a new challenge that didn't exist when the original goals were determined. A good idea is to reevaluate what you are doing.

If your peers don't really understand why they are doing something, then that doubt becomes an easy way for apathy to creep into your organization. The best way for students to recommit is to simply review the goals that were established at the beginning of the year.

Simply ask the question, "How is this working for us?" This sparks dialogue that leads to modifying, eliminating, or adding another goal. When students understand the *why*, the *how* is always easier to execute.

Tip #2: Make meetings fun again.

As a former advisor and student leader, I remember when meetings were no longer fun. Students began making excuses for not showing up. People began watching the time more than what was happening in the meeting. And, of course, they started asking, "Do we really have to meet this week?" If this sounds familiar, your meetings could be in need of some remodeling.

The first rule of thumb for meetings is that people must see a reason for them. If you don't have a good reason to meet, then more than likely you run the risk of members attending with bad attitudes and resentment, which often leads to apathy. An easy cure is to have a definite purpose for meeting.

Don't just meet to share information. Instead, get members to be active participants.

While some meetings are just routine, adding weekly assignments can make them exciting for everyone. For example:

☑ Assign a student to provide an ice breaker at the beginning of the meeting, like a funny story, a joke, or anything positive.

☑ Assign someone to be the note keeper.

☑ Have a show-and-tell so members get to know each other.

☑ Provide a cultural snack to educate each other about diversity.

☑ Give away a weekly award with a theme (peer nomination is the best idea).

☑ Hold a raffle for those who come to the meeting on time.

The best way to get the most out of the above ideas is to involve your peers. Be sure to make them part of the meeting by including them on the agenda, and let them know beforehand.

I had an advisor who started the meeting with a motivational quote. He would ask what we thought it meant, and he would then explain the relevance of the quote for the week. We always left the meeting feeling wiser.

For any meetings deemed as unnecessary, use technology to help disseminate information, like email, Facebook, Twitter, text, or whatever your students check regularly. This shows students that you value their time and that you expect them to be full participants in face-to-face meetings.

When you find ways to reassess your goals, restructure your meetings, and make them fun again, you begin the process of re-energizing your students in no time at all.

Things to Consider

1. How do you plan to hold other members accountable?

2. What are three things you can do to improve your organization's image?

   a)
   b)
   c)

3. If two members aren't getting along, how do you see your role as improving the situation?

CHAPTER 17

Accounting for Accountability

"When it comes to privacy and accountability, people always demand the former for themselves and the latter for everyone else." David Brin

There is no better time to learn about responsibility than as a student leader in college. However, knowing about accountability and actually using accountability principles in a student group are two very different things. Now we'll discuss how to implement an effective accountability system in your organization with three very useful tips you need to implement to get the most from your team members.

Tip #1: Clearly define job roles.

It is impossible to be accountable if you are not aware of your responsibilities. The first step to creating an organization based on accountability is to talk about expectations for each person's job.

Gather everyone with a specified position and have a conversation about what each person should expect to do in his or her role. For example, if you are the treasurer of an academic honors club, your group may decide that your responsibilities include collecting dues, keeping financial records, paying for supplies, and overseeing fundraising.

Once you have talked about roles and responsibilities, write down the job functions you have decided upon. Make sure everyone has a copy of what their job entails. It's important to create a list of job responsibilities for everyone involved in the upper echelons of a student organization, including faculty advisors and also the president of the organization.

Create a system of consequences for any job that is performed poorly. For example, if everyone agrees that a person repeatedly fails to meet their job expectations, they will be asked to leave that role.

Tip #2: Self-accountability.

For an organization to function at its best, it is vital that each person takes their responsibilities seriously. Of course, that means striving to meet every aspect of the job description that has been laid out for your role. Part of doing your best is holding yourself accountable for all of your actions.

Take credit for your successes, but more importantly, admit to your failures. Accepting responsibility makes it easier to pinpoint when something goes wrong, which overall helps to develop a better functioning organization.

Tip #3: Hold others accountable.

One role that every student leader should have is to enforce accountability principles. This means holding other group members responsible for their actions and talking about failures if they don't live up to job expectations.

It can be difficult to approach your peers and tell them they have not performed well in a job. But despite the inherent discomfort of the situation, as a student leader it is crucial that you approach them in a straightforward manner about their performance and with any concerns.

Always treat team members with respect when discussing their actions with them. Holding others accountable is never an excuse for meanness. To ensure that your criticism is constructive, use "I" phrases when talking about job responsibilities.

For example, if your club secretary hasn't been taking notes as laid out in the job description, say something like, "I have not gotten minutes lately," and definitely avoid something like, "You have not done a good job."

That type of comment is perceived as negative, and that you blame your colleague and are not giving constructive advice. Be firm but objective when you approach members about their job problems.

You may want to schedule frequent meetings with club organizers to ensure that expectations are talked about on a regular basis. This way, it won't seem like you are singling out any one person for poor performance. While it's important to hold everyone accountable, it's also critical that you do not foster bad feelings.

With regular one-on-one meetings, you give everyone positive feedback along with suggestions for improvement, and no one person will feel like a scapegoat for an organization's problems.

Finally, don't be afraid to impose negative consequences if a member's poor performance continues after many discussions. Following through and doing something about repeated failure is a big part of accountability. With a strong accountability system in place, your organization becomes more effective.

Things to Consider

1. What things can you do to keep your organization motivated?

2. What's the best part about being in this organization?

3. What system of accountability will you put in place?

CHAPTER 18

Utilizing Campus Resources to Help Your Organization

"Life is constantly providing us with new funds, new resources, even when we are reduced to immobility. In life's ledger there is no such thing as frozen assets. "
Henry Miller

Although you are ultimately responsible for making the most of your time in school, you're not working towards your degree alone. It takes everyone who works at the university to help the students get their education.

As a student leader, you will be helping other students make the most of the collegiate experience as well. Your responsibility is to assist your peers when they need it, to ensure that they have a comfortable home on campus, and to support their success at school, so that they may move forward in life and prepare for their futures.

One of the best ways that you can help your fellow students is to educate them about the resources on campus. Let's examine some of the most important resources that are available to you and your fellow students.

Advisors

The most obvious resource is your campus **advisor**. Every student has an advisor, yet not every student realizes just how helpful an advisor can be. Your advisor is available to give you feedback that will help you to make the best choices during your time at school, so make sure to make use of your advisor; he or she is one of the most valuable resources that is available.

It's always best to try to establish a good

relationship with your advisor as early as possible in your collegiate career. Invest a little time in getting to know your advisor a bit before you're in need of assistance, rather than waiting until you have to speak to him or her. This can help you avoid many problems later when you're actually seeking advice.

Your advisor's job is to help you make important decisions that affect not only your years in school, but potentially what happens in your life after you've graduated. Therefore, make the most of the opportunity to speak with your advisor whenever you're in need of such assistance.

Residence Life/Resident Assistants

If you live on a residential campus, you can also make use of your **Residence Life** staff as well. Your team of **Resident Assistants** (RAs) will be able to provide a lot of support, because they've got a great deal of insight about what some people experience as students on campus. Student leaders are also often resident assistants. Because of this dual role, they have a greater understanding of issues that other students face and, therefore, are well-equipped to help those who need it.

Don't be afraid to partner with Residence Life staff in order to help iron out issues that your organization may face. RAs often work on programming and have a certain buy-in with their existing relationships. These people work with students, assisting many types of people each day; thus, this is a team of students that can be very useful for you and your organization. It is never too late or too early to establish a good relationship with your RAs.

Career Services

As student leader, you will need to be in contact with **Career Services** during various times of the year. The latter part of the year is a time when your interaction with Career Services will prove to be especially vital, as this is the point when many graduating students will be job hunting.

Career Services can assist you all through the year, as well to help students find jobs or internships throughout the school year. They are also well-versed in ways to help students prepare for job-seeking outside of the university by assisting with résumé building and conducting mock interviews. Establishing a partnership with this particular office can be especially effective for your organization, as the staff there can also assist you in programming to educate students about these topics.

Financial Aid

Virtually every college student can use some extra money. One of **Financial Aid**'s biggest goals is to assist students in seeking additional funds for their education. Therefore, programs which deal with student finances can really benefit your organization as well as the student body as a whole.

Consider holding some financial events for the students. Invite financial experts to your campus and have representatives from banks conduct educational seminars to provide the students with helpful information. Hosting such programs will be invaluable to help students to manage their funds as well as to develop much-needed life skills, such as finding an apartment, opening a bank account, and maintaining a good credit score. It would be a great idea to include this programming in conjunction with Career Services as well as part of your leadership plans.

Other Campus Organizations

Other departments, like the Honors Department, ROTC, Food Services, Student Unions (if you are not SGA), and the Alumni Association, can all be instrumental in providing help for a variety of interesting programming. Additionally, these departments can also help students connect to outside resources, which may be of help to them in the future.

Your group can also seek other organizations as partners in programming. Your goal should not be outdoing one another; instead, focus on working together as a team. Every organization on campus has the same basic goal: to benefit the students.

By partnering with other organizations, you will be greatly increasing your scope in providing students with access to information. Even if relations between the two organizations have not always been extremely positive in the past, there is never a bad time to try enhancing relationships with other groups on campus.

While seeking assistance for your organization or for your university's students as a whole, you shouldn't feel as though you're working alone. Don't be afraid to look around and ask others for ideas. There are plenty of organizations, both large and small, who will be ready to pitch in and lend a hand in support of your mission to help prepare the students for a great future.

Things to Consider

1. What faculty, staff, or administrators do you currently have a relationship with?

2. How can they help you reach your organizational goals?

3. What upcoming campus events will require campus resources?

4. What campus resources will be required to execute large-scale events?

5. What campus resources do you plan to utilize this year?

CHAPTER 19

Leaving a Lasting Legacy

"We must become the change we want to see."
Mahatma Gandhi

A leader's legacy is sometimes defined by what they have done when they are no longer present on campus, not by what they accomplished while they were there.

One of the biggest mistakes many graduating student leaders make is not utilizing their position as an opportunity to mentor rising student leaders.

One of the best ways to mentor rising campus leaders is to help them gain experience. If your mentees are not given an opportunity to lead at some level, how can they become effective campus leaders?

While the next administration may have their own ideas of how to lead the campus, your challenge as the incumbent leader is to help guide and nurture future campus leaders. This is critical because it will define your legacy.

The reason that many world systems don't change very often is because the ideas were put in place by great thinkers and leaders. Ideas rule the world, not people.

What ideas are you putting in the minds of your mentees? If your mentees adopt your best and brightest ideas, you are sure to have a lasting legacy.

Here are some ideas to help give peer mentees an opportunity to lead:

☑ Give them a chance to run meetings and provide feedback after each meeting.

☑ Provide them with an opportunity to work on a big project. Don't give them all of the responsibility, but do allow them to contribute and observe what you are doing. This will allow them to stay engaged in the process and not feel overwhelmed.

☑ Create and role-play "what-if scenarios." For example: "What would you do if a member is not giving 100 percent to the organization?" "What would you do if you have two members who refuse to work together?" Allow them to present their ideas and answers, as well as offer insight on how to handle certain situations.

☑ If you cannot attend an important event, allow them to go in your absence. This way, they get the experience and know-how to conduct themselves the next time.

☑ Help them find their personal leadership style. Ask them questions about how they plan to run the show and why they plan to run it that way.

Implement these ideas and you are sure to cultivate a leader and leave a legacy, all at the same time.

Things to Consider

1. Looking forward, what would you like to be remembered for, and how do you want to be remembered?

2. How do you intend to create and mentor rising student leaders?

CHAPTER 20

Moving Forward

"Life can only be understood backwards; but it must be lived forwards." Soren Kierkegaard

As the end of the school year fast approaches, it's time to look at what's ahead. Being a student leader presents several great opportunities, but being a college student is your first priority. Depending on your year (pre-college, first year, sophomore, junior or senior), you have much to consider. The following tips will help you prepare for each next step as you move from pre-college toward college graduation and beyond.

Pre-College

Congratulations! You have been accepted and are on your way to college! But before your first step on campus, take a minute to get organized. Do you have all of the necessary paperwork: college acceptance letter, financial aid award letters, immunization shot records, housing assignment letter, transcripts?

Be mindful that your selected college may receive thousands of applications, and there is a great possibility that your paperwork could get lost. The way to remedy this problem is to keep your paperwork organized and accessible.

As an incoming first-year student, your first step to having a successful college experience is to get connected with campus resources. If you can visit the campus before your official move-in date, take that opportunity. Doing so allows you to get connected and stay connected. It also eliminates or greatly reduces any issues. I highly recommend visiting these offices **before** your move-in date:

☑ Financial Aid

☑ Residence Life/Housing (and your future residence hall)

☑ Health Services

☑ Your Advisor

☑ Admissions

☑ Registrar

☑ Student Support Service Offices

☑ Library

☑ Student Life/Campus Activities

First-Year Students

As you move toward your sophomore year, it's time to start thinking about your major. You may not know it yet, and that's okay. However, it's important to begin taking electives that will help you determine your major. It's also the time to get connected with resources such as:

☑ Service Learning

☑ Career Services

☑ Student Life/Campus Activities

☑ Study Aboard

☑ Tutorial Services

☑ All Major Departments

All of these provide a more enriched college experience and clues to your career field.

Sophomore Students

Now that you have survived the sophomore slump, it's time to decide on what you plan to do next. If you haven't yet declared a major, this is a good time to do so. If you still need time consider summer school, or a summer job in a field of interest, or during the first half of your junior year.

While I don't believe in picking a major for the sake of choosing, it's important to remember that college graduation is the key. You may never find a job in your declared major, but having a college degree will open up more doors than just having college credits.

Furthermore, as a sophomore you will need to start being more intentional about internships. The more intentional you are, the more clarity you will have regarding your intended major, as well as your career choice.

Junior Students

You are so close to graduation that you can see it. As you rapidly approach the big day, there are still some loose ends you must tie up.

First, have you visited Career Services and taken advantage of their services (mock interviews, resume writing workshops, job database)? No matter what you decide on, this is a good place to acquire tools to help you land a job upon graduation.

Secondly, perhaps getting a job after college doesn't interest you. If not, have you started thinking about the possibility of graduate school, professional school, serving in the military, volunteering in the peace corps, or some other alternative?

Weighing your options now gives you time to take the necessary tests, to acquire recommendations, and to raise your GPA so that you are in a more favorable position.

Senior Students

You have fought the good fight and now it's time to enter the gates of the real world. As you attempt to make a smooth transition from undergraduate to college graduate, you need to consider the interim. So before getting your tassel, consider these questions:

☑ Where do you plan to live after graduation?

☑ How do you plan to provide for yourself during this time?

☑ Do you have a back-up plan?

☑ If you do have a place to stay and a way to provide for yourself, how will you make the most of your time?

☑ Now that you have finished school, what's your next major goal, and what's the time line for achieving that major goal?

I know, you just finished and want some time to rest on your laurels. And that's fine. But just remember: If you are not striving, you are sliding!

It's time to begin a new phase of your life, whether you like it or not. That's part of change and progress. Change has a way of inviting itself into each person's daily life. The best way to deal with it is to accept it, embrace it, and prepare for it in the best way you can.

<u>Things to Consider</u>

1. What are some lessons you have learned this year?

2. Of the lessons learned, what has changed your life in a profound way?

APPENDIX 1

Program Ideas/Student Issues By Month

FALL SEMESTER

August/September	Student Issues
Adult Literacy Awareness	Adjustment
Jazz	Roommate Conflicts
Library Card Sign-Up	Residence Halls/Room Change
National Chicken	Academics/Finances
National Piano	Emotional
National School Success	Social Rejection
Self-Improvement	Community Agreements/Service
National Cholesterol	Time Management
Education & Awareness	Homesickness
Classical Music	Campus Familiarization
International Visitors	Alcohol and Drugs
National Honey	International Student
National Courtesy	Hall Council Involvement
National Rice	Long-distance Relationships
Pleasure Your Mate	Computer Access/Usage
Women of Achievement	Policies and Procedures
National Alcohol & Drug	Values Exploration-Personal
Treatment	Beliefs
Hispanic Heritage	
911 Remembrance	
Hurricane Katrina	

FALL SEMESTER

October	Student Issues
American Magazine	Alcohol Issues
Computer Learning	Roommate Conflict-Privacy &
Crime Prevention	"Stuff"
Ending Hunger	Health & Fitness
Fire Prevention	Personal Safety
Hunger Awareness	Time Conflicts between
Lupus Awareness	Academics & Social
National AIDS Awareness	Relationships: Dating and Non-
National Car Care	dating, Student Withdrawal –
National Education	Adjustment
National Popcorn Poppin'	Friendship
Polish-American Heritage	Judicial Process
National Seafood	Advance Enrollment Planning
Hispanic Heritage	Disenchantment with School
Italian-American Heritage	Academics – Midterms
& Culture	Study Skills
Auto Battery Safety	Values Exploration – Sexuality
Consumer Information	Homesickness (Homecoming)
National Domestic	Job Panic for Mid-year Grads
Violence Awareness	Group Identity
Healthy Lung	Problems
International Book Fair	Financial Strain
Vegetarian Awareness	Involvement Opportunities
Lesbian & Gay History	Room Reassignments
Lock-in Safety	Halloween
National Breast Cancer	
National Dessert	
National Pasta	
National Pizza	
National Pork	
Value of Play	
National Disability	

FALL SEMESTER

November/Dec.	Student Issues
Good Nutrition	Finals/Grades
National Diabetes	Changing Relationships
National Epilepsy	Friends from Home
Awareness	Significant Others
World AIDS Day	Parents
National Philately	Time Management Conflicts
Religion & Philosophy	Economic Anxieties
Books	Roommate Problems – Short
Latino American	Tempers
Peanut Butter Lover's	Holiday Break Plans
Native American Heritage	Depression
International Creative	Results of Procrastination
Child & Adult	Stress
	Social Apathy
	Problems Related to Alcohol
	Health Issues

SPRING SEMESTER

January	Student Issues
Crime Stoppers	Academics
Soup	Post-holiday Depression
Volunteer Blood Donor	Roommate Relationships
National Eye Care	Community Agreements
Hot Tea	Revisited
Oatmeal	Involvement
Martin Luther King Jr.	Leadership
Day	Social/Academic Balance
	Family Loss/Stress
	New Environment
	New Residents
	Weight Gain
	Health Issues
	Money Problems
	Human Diversity

SPRING SEMESTER

February	Student Issues
African American History	Cabin Fever
Canned Food	Summer Job Hunting
World Understanding	Graduation Planning
Creative Romance	Cleanliness in Common Areas
National Blah-Buster	Interpersonal Communication
Humpback Whales	Living Arrangements for Fall
Awareness	Tutoring Services
International Boost Your	Race Issues
Self-Esteem	Sexuality Issues – Safe Sex
American History	Romance & Dating
American Heart	Alcohol & Relationships
National Condom	Depression
Black History	Where to Study
National Snack Food	
National Weddings	

SPRING SEMESTER

March	Student Issues
American Red Cross	Safe Spring Break
National Frozen Food	Travel Tips
National Peanut	Alcohol
Irish-American Heritage	Goal Setting – Choosing a Major
National Nutrition	Existential Crises for Seniors
National Women's History	Was My Education Worth Anything?
	Did I Choose the Wrong Major?
	Job Interview Anxiety for Seniors
	Women's Issues
	Values Clarification
	Career Services
	What Now?
	Resume Writing
	Resume Building
	Summer Job Hunting
	Money for Spring Break

SPRING SEMESTER

April	Student Issues
Keep America Beautiful	Health Issues
Listening Awareness	Sexual Assault Issues as Weather
Multicultural	Becomes Nicer
Communication	Food Service Concerns
National Recycling	Financial Strain Affects Social
National STDs Education	Life
& Awareness	Community Issues
Actors Appreciation	Noise as Weather Gets Warmer
Alcohol Awareness	Public Trash Issues
National Anxiety	Time Management
National Humor	Mating Season
National Poetry	Pressure of Selecting a Major
Stress Awareness	Illness due to Weather Changes

SPRING SEMESTER

May	Student Issues
Better Sleep	Take Back the Night
Electrical Safety	Closure for Communities
Mental Health	Closing Procedures
National Barbecue	Year is Ending
National Hamburger	Finals Pressure
National Egg	Worry about Going Home for
National High Blood	the Summer
Pressure	Health & Fitness
Asian/Pacific American	Academics
Heritage	Frustration
Revise Your Work Schedule	Disappointment
National Sasquatch	Senior Job Panic
Month of Peace	Moving
National Asparagus	Depression
National Bike	Separation Anxiety
National Mime	
National Physical Fitness	
& National Photo Sports	
National Strawberry	
Personal History	
Awareness	
Cinco de Mayo (Mexico)	
National Salad	

SPRING SEMESTER

June	Student Issues
Fresh Fruits & Vegetables	Paying for Summer School
Fireworks Safety	Transferring Credit
National Accordion	Transitioning into Career
Awareness	Gaining Meaningful Summer
National Drive Safe	Experiences
National Pest Control	
Supreme Court Month of	
Tough Decisions	
Gay Pride	
Black Music	
Tony Award	
June Dairy	
Youth Suicide Prevention	
Zoo & Aquarium	

APPENDIX 2

Creative Programs on a Shoestring Budget

No matter the size of your organization, here is a list of programs that you can implement regardless of your budget:

☑ Ask a business professor or money management guru to give a lecture on personal finances.

☑ Host a potluck dinner with professors.

☑ Host an old school Saturday morning cartoons breakfast.

☑ Co-sponsor a résumé writing clinic with the office of Career Services.

☑ Co-sponsor a mock interview clinic with the office of Career Services.

☑ Host a workshop on how to build and improve your credit score conducted with a finance expert.

- ☑ Hold a graduate student meet and greet forum where students relate what they wish they had known earlier about graduate school.
- ☑ Rent the gym and do a basketball or other type of sports tournament.
- ☑ Collect canned goods for the less fortunate and donate them to a food drop.
- ☑ Have a residential hall decoration contest.
- ☑ Have a building decoration contest in conjunction with homecoming.
- ☑ Hold an ice cream social.
- ☑ Host a study break; serve coffee and cake.
- ☑ Host a healthy study break; serve healthy foods and offer nutrition lists.
- ☑ Ask a physical education/health faculty member to talk about weight training, training for a marathon, or healthy eating.
- ☑ Host a cooking contest like "Top Chef" or chili cooking contest or a desert sampling.
- ☑ Do an artist cover, like Lady Gaga, Michael Jackson, or another popular artist.
- ☑ Hold a fashion show with or without a twist.

- ☑ Replicate a popular TV show like "American Idol" or "The Voice."
- ☑ Hold relationship forums where men and women talk about relationship issues.
- ☑ Sponsor a series of computer learning clinics where people can learn basic and advanced software skills.
- ☑ Host a field day.
- ☑ Host an arts & crafts night.
- ☑ Host a karaoke night.
- ☑ Hold a discussion forum about a controversial movie, book, topic, or other current events hosted by a professor or fan of that topic.
- ☑ Host a lock-in, out-all-night event where students participate in activities overnight.
- ☑ Hold a marathon dance competition.
- ☑ Host a 10K run on campus.
- ☑ Provide community service at a local shelter or a church.
- ☑ Provide alternative programming on Friday and Saturday nights.

- ☑ Sponsor a particular team on a sports night and wear team colors, or have a funny hat night at sports home games.
- ☑ On Halloween night or Christmas invite the local community to your campus and have faculty/staff members dress for the occasion.
- ☑ Hire a diversity lecturer.
- ☑ Hire a leadership expert.
- ☑ Host a passport drive where people can apply for a passport.
- ☑ Host an international fair, festival, and/or parade.
- ☑ Host a video game tournament.

These are just some ideas for a shoestring budget that could be implemented and work well on most campuses. Use your creativity and that of your organization to add to this list.

ABOUT THE AUTHOR

 Tawan Perry, M.Ed., is a student leadership expert and an award winning author. As an undergraduate student, he served as both SGA Vice President and as a resident assistant. After graduating from college, he worked at various institutions as a housing administrator, Greek advisor, and assistant dean.

Today, Tawan is a nationally renowned student leadership expert who has been featured in various magazines, talk shows, and printed media. He currently resides in Raleigh, N.C. For more information visit www.tawanperry.com

More Products from College Success Expert, Tawan Perry!

College Sense: What College and High School Advisors Don't Tell You about College

Making sense of higher education can confound the most stellar of students. Your college education isn't just about gaining knowledge, but an experience unlike any other you will have in life. Navigating the college environment is about learning the language: If you know how the system works, you can understand and prepare for the complexities that college presents.

It explores a myriad of essential topics such as how to reduce and eliminate debt, the questions that you should ask during your campus visit, and how to get the most of your college experience. It's the only book you'll ever need to help you prepare for all those things that your advisors didn't tell you about college. **College Sense was the 2008 National Best Books award winner for college guides.**

College Sense is ideal for:

☑ Any incoming first year student

☑ High school or PTA that want to give graduating seniors an invaluable gift

☑ Any community college student that will be transferring into a 4-year institution

☑ Non-profit organizations that want to give students an advantage in college

☑ University 101 college course textbook

College Sense for Parents

Each year college becomes gradually more expensive, and families find themselves desperately looking for ways to reduce rising costs. *College Sense for Parents* offers help by providing several time-tested strategies that will eliminate debt and reduce the cost of college. This audio recording covers topics such as how to reduce the cost of tuition, board, books, application fees, and other related college expenses. Listen to it on your way to work or in the comfort of your home. *College Sense for Parents* gets straight to the point and offers tips that will easily save you thousands of dollars. This is a **must have** for any parent with college bound children.

Quote These (College Edition)

Whether you are an incoming freshmen or a procrastinating senior, *Quote These* is the most astounding book of quotes ever assembled to assist and inspire college students. Categorized by such themes as transition, relationships and time management, this book is a great resource whether you're writing speeches, personal statements, essays, or just looking for guidance during those often riddle filled college years.

Students Go to College For Free: How to Get a B.S. without the B.S.

kindle edition

If you're stressed out about how to pay for your college education or looking for a way to get your degree without going into a lifetime of debt, *Students Go to College For Free* has the solution. A **must read** book for students at all levels, advisors and counselors too, this book shows you how to attend a tuition-free college, attend prestigious schools without the ACT or SAT, get your master's degree and doctorate for free, pay in-state tuition even if you're out of state, and how to earn 30 or more college credits before taking a college class.

14166309R00073

Made in the USA
Charleston, SC
24 August 2012